The Private Journal Of A Journey From Boston To New York: In The Year 1704

Sarah Kemble Knight

In the interest of creating a more extensive selection of rare historical book reprints, we have chosen to reproduce this title even though it may possibly have occasional imperfections such as missing and blurred pages, missing text, poor pictures, markings, dark backgrounds and other reproduction issues beyond our control. Because this work is culturally important, we have made it available as a part of our commitment to protecting, preserving and promoting the world's literature. Thank you for your understanding.

THE

PRIVATE JOURNAL

OF A

Journey from Boston to New York,

IN

THE YEAR 1704.

KEPT BY

MADAM KNIGHT.

ALBANY:
FRANK H. LITTLE.
1865.

PREFACE.

In the month of October, 1704, Madam Sarah Knight traveled on horseback from Boston to New Haven. She continued her journey to New York in the following December, and after staying there two weeks returned to New Haven, and thence in March to Boston. During this time she kept a journal, which was for many years preserved among her descendants, but now is believed to be lost. This journal was published in New York in 1825, and in the introduction to that edition it is stated that "the original orthography has been carefully preserved." The present edition is an exact reprint of the former, including the introduction, with the addition of a few notes.

Madam Sarah Knight was born April 19, 1666. She was the daughter of Capt. Thomas

Kemble, a merchant of Boston, and of Elizabeth Trarice, his wife.[1] He was a native of Great Britain, and resided in Charlestown as early as 1651, and for several years afterwards.[2] For many years he was an attorney or agent of Mr. Robert Rich, a merchant of London.[3] He had several children, one of whom, John, a cooper or carpenter, died in New York, and by a will made in 1695, gave his lands and houses to his wife for her life, then to Madam Knight for her life, and then to her daughter.[1]

Before the birth of Sarah, Capt. Kemble had moved to Boston; and there in 1676 he built a large house on the easterly side of Moon street, corner of Moon street court, about half way from Sun Court street to Fleet street. The house was demolished in 1832, or soon after, and a tobacco warehouse erected, which has now been con-

---

[1] Savage's *Genealogical Dictionary*, III, 21, *et seq.*

[2] Littell's *Living Age*, LVII, 964; a very full and interesting article, by Mr. William R. Deane, who has gathered nearly all the facts that are known about Madam Knight, and has kindly permitted their use. Much of this preface is taken from that article, which is referred to, for convenience, by his initials.

[3] W. R. D.

verted into the Catholic church.[1] He lived in this house until his death, January 29, 1688-9. His wife survived him until December 19, 1712. The grave stones of both are in the Copp's Hill burying ground.[2]

Sarah Kemble was married to Richard Knight of Boston, "a Captain of a London trader."[3] He died abroad, but in what year is not ascertained. Mr. Deane says that his wife supposed him to be living in 1706, when she signed as his attorney;[4] but the notice in the *Historical Magazine*, just referred to, states that her journey in 1704 was to claim some of his property in New York.

The fact that he is not mentioned in the journal seems to favor the latter of these views. He had had a former wife, Remember Grafton, the daughter of Nathaniel Grafton, of Salem;[1] and he is said by one authority to have been "bred a carver."[5]

Soon after her return from the New York

---

[1] *Historical Magazine*, ix, 93, *et seq.*
[2] W. R. D.
[3] *Historical Magazine*, ix, 93, *et seq.*
[4] W. R. D., referring to Middlesex Reg. Deeds, iii, 463.
[5] Savage's *Genealogical Dictionary*.

journey Madam Knight opened a school for children. Dr. Franklin and Dr. Samuel Mather were among her scholars. As she was the only surviving child of her parents she continued to keep school in the house built by her father until 1714. She then sold the estate to Peter Papillion; and it became afterwards the property of Hannah, wife of Dr. Samuel Mather. In the year 1763 Dr. Mather had the house new glazed; and one pane of glass was preserved as a curiosity till it was lost when Charlestown was burnt in 1765. That pane bore the following lines written with a diamond:

> Through many toils and many frights
> I have returned, poor Sarah Knights
> Over great rocks and many stones
> God has preserved from fractured bones.

It was as a schoolmistress that she acquired the title of Madam; and she is said to have been noted for teaching composition.[1]

Elizabeth, the only child of Madam Knight,

---

[1] *Historical Magazine*, as cited above. In his autobiography Dr. Franklin does not mention Madam Knight; but he states that he was sent to the grammar school at eight years of age; and this would correspond with the time when Madam Knight gave up her school.

was born in Boston, May 8th, 1689, and was married there by Dr. Increase Mather to Colonel John Livingston of New London, Oct. 1st, 1713.[1] She was his second wife. His first wife was met by Madam Knight and is mentioned in the journal. Mrs. Elizabeth Livingston survived her husband; but had no children. A table of freestone with this inscription perpetuates her memory:

> "Interd vnder this stone is the body of Madam Elizabeth Livingston, relict of Col. John Livingstone of New London, who departed this life March 17th A. D. 1735-6 in the 48th year of her age."[2]

It was undoubtedly the marriage of her daughter which induced Madam Knight to sell her house. About this time she removed to the neighborhood of Norwich and New London, Ct., and there spent the remainder of an energetic and active life.

[1] W. R. D.
[2] Miss Frances M. Caulkins's *History of New London*, 365. Many of the subsequent details of Madam Knight's life, after she removed from Boston, are copied by permission from Miss Caulkins' History, and from a letter written by her to Mr. Deane in 1858, and printed in the article already mentioned.

In 1717 a silver cup for the communion service was presented by her to the church in Norwich; and the town by vote, August 12th, gave her liberty to "sit in the pew where she used to sit."[1] In 1718, March 26th, Madam Knight and six other persons were presented in one indictment " for selling strong drink to the Indians." They were fined twenty shillings and costs. It is added to the record, " Mrs. Knight accused her maid, Ann Clark, of the fact." After this period Madam Knight appears as a land purchaser in the North Parish of New London, generally as a partner with Joseph Bradford. Col. Livingston had purchased a great amount of land from the Mohegan Indians, which he had gradually parted with. Madam Knight and Mr. Bradford repurchased much of this land. One deed conveyed to them more than two thousand acres for which they paid £1000; and another deed was for about half that extent.

She was also a pew holder in the new church

[1] In those early days places were assigned, or, as the phrase was, "the meeting house was seated" by the authority of the town. The "chief seats in the synagogues" were matters of great interest and ambition and sometimes of much controversy.

built in the North Parish of New London about 1724, and was sometimes styled of Norwich and sometimes of New London. She retained her dwelling house in Norwich; but her farms where she spent a portion of her time, were within the bounds of New London. On one of these, the Livingston farm, upon the Norwich road, she kept entertainment for travelers, and is called innkeeper. At this place she died, Sept. 25th, 1727, and was brought to New London for interment. A gray headstone, of which an exact impression is given on a following page, marks the place.[1] The only child of Madam Knight, Elizabeth, relict of Col. John Livingston, survived her, and presented her inventory, which comprised two farms in Mohegan with housing and mills, £1600, and estate in Norwich, £210.

The journal which is here reprinted, had been carefully preserved in manuscript in the Christophers family, to whom it came after the death of Mr. Livingston; Sarah, wife of Christopher Christophers, who was a Prout, of

[1] Miss Caulkins's *History of New London*, 372, et seq.

New-Haven, and a relative, being appointed to administer on her estate. From a descendant of this Mrs. Christophers, viz: Mrs. Ichabod Wetmore, of Middletown, the manuscript was obtained for publication. It had been neatly copied into a small book.[1] The original was not returned to Mrs. Wetmore, and, with the exception of a single leaf, has unfortunately been destroyed.[2]

Madam Knight's business on this journey was, as she says, the distribution of an estate and one evidently in which she had a personal interest. It may possibly have been that of her brother John, who had died in New York a few years previously, or perhaps that of her husband, as stated by Mrs. Hannah Mather Crocker.[3] A suggestion has been made that it was the estate of Caleb Trowbridge; but this is not probable, as her name appears in 1704 as a

---

[1] Miss Caulkins's *History of New London*, 373.

[2] It appears from Mr. Deane's article that this leaf was then in possession of Mr. Theodore Dwight of New York, who edited the journal.

[3] *Historical Magazine*, IX, 93.

witness to the papers by which that estate was settled.[1]

It is evident from her journal that Madam Knight was energetic and observing; that she had some imagination and a good perception of the ludicrous. She seems also to have been free from that strict and narrow character which is generally attributed to the Puritan of early New England. She rides a few miles on Sunday, and considers the prohibition of "innocent merriment among young people," to be "rigid." She makes jokes on Mr. Devil's name, which, only a few years earlier, might have convicted her of witchcraft, if they had come to the ears of Cotton Mather. And although absent from home for five months, and a visitor with at least two or three clergymen, she gives no account of any sermon which she may have heard. Her silence in this particular may have been because there was more novelty in the matters which she narrates.

Wherever it is possible to make the test, her journal will be found accurate even in slight

[1] W. R. D.

matters. It may therefore with good reason be relied upon in all its details.

In the introduction to the former edition it is said that over the same journey which Madam Knight made, " we proceed at our ease without exposure, and almost without fatigue, in a day and a half." A penciled note made in 1849 to a copy of the edition adds: " now performed by rail road in ten hours." That time is now reduced to eight. One may venture to think that the speed of travel will never be carried to a much higher degree than it has now reached.

Albany, 1865.

THE
PRIVATE JOURNAL
KEPT BY
MADAM KNIGHT,
ON A JOURNEY
FROM BOSTON TO NEW YORK,
IN THE YEAR 1704.

FROM THE ORIGINAL MANUSCRIPT.

INTRODUCTION.

THIS is not a work of fiction, as the scarcity of old American manuscripts may induce some to imagine; but it is a faithful copy from a diary in the author's own hand-writing, compiled soon after her return home, as it appears, from notes recorded daily while on the road. She was a resident of Boston, and a lady of uncommon literary attainments, as well as of great taste and strength of mind. She was called Madam Knight, out of respect to her character, according to a custom once common in New England; but what was her family name the publishers have not been able to discover.

The object proposed in printing this little work is not only to please those who have partially studied the progressive history of our country, but to direct the attention of others to subjects of that description, unfashionable as they still are; and also to remind the public that documents, even as unpretending as the following, may possess a real value, if they contain facts which will be hereafter sought for to illustrate interesting periods in our history.

It is to be regretted that the brevity of the work should have allowed the author so little room for the display of the cultivated mind and the brilliant fancy which frequently betray themselves in the course of the narrative; and no one can rise from the perusal without wishing some happy chance might yet discover more full delineations of life and character from the same practiced hand. Subjects so closely connected with ourselves ought to excite a degree of curiosity and interest, while we are generally so ready to open our minds and our libraries to the most minute details of foreign governments, and the modes and men of distant countries, with which we can have only a collateral connection.

In copying the following work for the press, the original orthography has been carefully preserved, in some cases, it may be, so far as to retain the errors of the pen, for fear of introducing any unwarrantable modernism. The punctuation was very hasty, and therefore has not been regarded. Two interruptions occur in the original near the commencement, which could not be supplied; and in a few instances it has been thought proper to make short omissions, but none of them materially affect the narrative.

The reader will find frequent occasion to compare the state of things in the time of our author with that of the present period, particularly with regard to the number of the inhabitants, and the facilities and accommodations prepared for travelers. Over that tract of country where she traveled about a fortnight on horseback, under the direction of a hired guide, with frequent risks of life and limb, and sometimes without food or shelter for many miles, we proceed at our ease, without exposure and almost without fatigue, in a day and a half, through a well peopled land, supplied with good stage coaches and public houses, or the still greater luxuries of the elegant steam boats which daily traverse our waters.

THE

JOURNAL

OF

MADAM KNIGHT.

Monday, Octb'r. y⁰ second, 1704.—About three o'clock afternoon, I begun my Journey from Boston to New Haven; being about two Hundred Mile. My Kinsman, Capt. Robert Luist,¹ waited on me as farr as Dedham, where I was to meet yᵉ Western post.²

¹ Robert Luist, shopkeeper of Charlestown, with others, signed a receipt for his share of Mrs. Livingston's estate. Miss Caulkins's letter, W. R. D. In Savage's *Genealogical Dictionary* this name is found under LEWIS.

² Letters patent, granting to Thomas Neale for twenty-one years the franchise of establishing a Post Office, were issued in 1691, and in 1693 the General Court of Massachusetts, under the authority of those letters, established a "General Letter Office."

The western post was the post between Boston and New York. A few years later, during the "winter months," it set out once a

I vissitted the Reverd. Mr. Belcher,[1] y̨ᵉ Minister of yᵉ town, and tarried there till evening, in hopes yᵉ post would come along. But he not coming, I resolved to go to Billingses where he used to lodg, being 12 miles further. But being ignorant of the way, Madᵐ Billings,[2] seing no persuasions of her good spouses or hers could prevail with me to Lodg there that night, Very kindly went wyth me to yᵉ Tavern, where I hoped to get my guide, And desired the Hostess to inquire of her guests whether any of them would go with mee. But they being tyed by the Lipps to a pewter engine, scarcely allowed themselves time to say what clownish * * * *

[*Here half a page of the MS. is gone.*]
* * * Peices of eight, I told her no, I would not be accessary to such extortion.

Then John shan't go, sais shee. No, indeed, shan't hee; And held forth at that rate a long

fortnight, going alternately to Saybrook and to Hartford, and at those places exchanging mails with the New York rider.

Mass. Hist. Col. 3d Series, XII, 48.

[1] The Rev. Joseph Belcher, who was graduated at Harvard in 1690 and ordained at Dedham Nov. 29, 1693.

[2] Probably a misprint for "Madam Belcher."

time, that I began to fear I was got among the Quaking tribe, beleeving not a Limbertong'd sister among them could outdo Madm. Hostes.

Upon this, to my no small surprise, son John arrose, and gravely demanded what I would give him to go with me? Give you, sais I, are you John? Yes, says he, for want of a Better, And behold! this John look't as old as my Host, and perhaps had bin a man in the last Century. Well, Mr. John, sais I, make your demands. Why, half a pss. of eight and a dram, sais John. I agreed, and gave him a Dram (now) in hand to bind the bargain.

My hostess catechis'd John for going so cheep, saying his poor wife would break her heart * *

[*Here another half page of the MS. is gone.*]
His shade on his Hors resembled a Globe on a Gate post. His habitt, Hors and furniture, its looks and goings Incomparably answered the rest.

Thus Jogging on with an easy pace, my Guide telling mee it was dangero's to Ride hard in the Night, (wh^ch his horse had the sence to avoid,) Hee entertained me with the Adventurs he had passed by late Rideing, and eminent Dangers he had escaped, so that, Remembring the Hero's in Parismus¹ and the Knight of the Oracle, I didn't know but I had mett wth a Prince disguis'd.

When we had Ridd about an how'r, wee come into a thick swamp, wch. by Reason of a great fogg, very much startled mee, it being now very Dark. But nothing dismay'd John: Hee had encountered a thousand and a thousand such Swamps, having a Universall Knowledge in the woods; and readily Answered all my inquiries wch. were not a few.

In about an how'r, or something more, after we left the Swamp, we come to Billinges, where I was to Lodg. My Guide dismounted and very Complasantly help't me down and shewd the door, signing to me wth his hand to Go in; wch I Gladly did—But had not gone many steps into

---

[1] Parismus, the renowned prince of Bohemia, his most famous, delectable and pleasant history; containing his noble battails brought against the Persians, his love to Laurana, the King's daughter of Thessaly, and his strange adventures in the desolate Island &c. London, T. Creede, 1598. Eighteen editions of it are recorded during the next hundred years. Written by Edward Ford.

the Room, ere I was Interogated by a young Lady I understood afterwards was the Eldest daughter of the family, with these, or words to this purpose, (viz.) Law for mee—what in the world brings You here at this time a night?—I never see a woman on the Rode so Dreadfull late, in all the days of my versall life. Who are You? Where are You going? I'me scar'd out of my witts—with much now of the same Kind. I stood aghast, Prepareing to reply, when in comes my Guide—to him Madam turn'd, Roreing out: Lawfull heart, John, is it You?—how de do! Where in the world are you going with this woman? Who is she? John made no Ansr. but sat down in the corner, fumbled out his black Junk, and saluted that instead of Debb; she then turned agen to mee and fell anew into her silly questions, without asking me to sitt down.

I told her she treated me very Rudely, and I did not think it my duty to answer her unmannerly Questions. But to get ridd of them, I told her I come there to have the post's company with me to-morrow on my Journey, &c. Miss star'd awhile, drew a chair, bid me sitt, And then run up stairs and putts on two or three Rings, (or else I had not seen them before,) and returning, sett herself just before me, showing the way to Reding,[1] that I might see her Ornaments, perhaps to gain the more respect. But her Granam's new Rung sow, had it appeared, would affected me as much. I paid honest John wth money and dram according to contract, and Dismist him, and pray'd Miss to shew me where I must Lodg. Shee conducted me to a parlour in a little back Lento,[2] wch was almost fill'd wth the bedsted, wch was so high I was forced to climb on a chair to gitt up to ye wretched bed that lay on it; on wch having Stretcht my tired Limbs, and lay'd my head on a Sad-colourd[3] pillow, I began to think on the transactions of ye past day.

Tuesday, October ye third, about 8 in the

[1] *In Notes and Queries*, 2d Series, vol. 6, p. 233, there is an inquiry as to the origin of this phrase, but it is unanswered.

[2] Lean to.

[3] Sombre, dark. "The colours are too sad." Beaumont and Fletcher, *Love's Cure*, Act III, Scene 2, Dyce's edition, vol. IX, p. 151.

morning, I with the Post proceeded forward without observing any thing remarkable; And about two, afternoon, Arrived at the Post's second stage, where the western Post mett^1 him and exchanged Letters. Here, having called for something to eat, ye woman bro't in a Twisted thing like a cable, but something whiter; and laying it on the bord, tugg'd for life to bring it into a capacity to spread; wch having wth great pains accomplished, shee serv'd in a dish of Pork and Cabage, I suppose the remains of Dinner. The sause was of a deep Purple, wch I tho't was boil'd in her dye Kettle; the bread was Indian, and every thing on the Table service Agreeable to these. I, being hungry, gott a little down; but my stomach was soon cloy'd, and what cabbage I swallowed serv'd me for a Cudd the whole day after.

Having here discharged the Ordnary for self and Guide, (as I understood was the custom,)

[1] The chief post office in Connecticut was New London, and this post was probably the rider from that place, who exchanged letters here and then returned to New London. Madam Knight went with him, and he thus became her "third guide."

About Three afternoon went on with my Third Guide, who Rode very hard: and having crossed Providence Ferry, we come to a River wch they Generally Ride thro'.[1] But I dare not venture; so the Post got a Ladd and Cannoo to carry me to tother side, and hee rid thro' and Led my hors. The Cannoo was very small and shallow, so that when we were in she seem'd redy to take in water, which greatly terrified mee, and caused me to be very circumspect, sitting with my hands fast on each side, my eyes stedy, not

---

[1] This must have been where the village of Pawtuxet now is. The route from Boston to New York through Rhode Island followed the shore of the bay and sea very nearly. From Providence it went through the present villages of Pawtuxet, Apponarg, East Greenwich, a little west of Wickford, then southerly through Tower Hill, Wakefield (formerly known as McCoon's Mills), and then southerly and westerly near the shore by Charlestown and westerly to Pawcatuc Bridge. It was long known as the Pequot path, road to Pequot and afterwards as the King's or Queen's Highway and the old Post road, and is throughout of greater width than the average country roads. A new road through the present towns of North and South Kingstown leading through the present village of Kingston was laid out 1703. See Potter's *History of Narraganset*. (*R. I. Hist. Soc. Coll*, III, 223). E. R. P.

This note and the others with these initials are from the pen of E. R. Potter, Esq. of Kingston, R. I.

daring so much as to lodg my tongue a hair's breadth more on one side of my mouth then tother, nor so much as think on Lott's wife, for a wry thought would have oversett our wherey; But was soon put out of this pain, by feeling the Cannoo on shore, wch I as soon almost saluted with my feet; and Rewarding my sculler, again mounted and made the best of our way forwards. The Rode here was very even and ye day pleasant, it being now near Sunsett. But the Post told mee we had neer 14 miles to Ride to the next Stage, (where we were to Lodg.) I askt him of the rest of the Rode, foreseeing wee must travail in the night. Hee told mee there was a bad River we were to Ride thro', wch was so very firce a hors could sometimes hardly stem it: But it was but narrow, and wee should soon be over. I cannot express The concern of mind this relation sett me in: no thoughts but those of the dang'ros River could entertain my Imagination, and they were as formidable as varios, still Tormenting me with blackest Ideas of my Approching fate — Sometimes seing myself drowning, otherwhiles drowned, and at the best like a holy

Sister Just come out of a Spiritual Bath in dripping Garments.

Now was the Glorious Luminary, wth his swift Coursers arrived at his Stage, leaving poor me wth the rest of this part of the lower world in darkness, with which *wee* were soon Surrounded. The only Glimering we now had was from the spangled Skies, Whose Imperfect Reflections rendered every Object formidable. Each lifeless Trunk, with its shatter'd Limbs, appear'd an Armed Enymie; and every little stump like a Ravenous devourer. Nor could I so much as discern my Guide, when at any distance, which added to the terror.

Thus, absolutely lost in Thought, and dying with the very thoughts of drowning, 1 come up wth the post, who I did not see till even with his Hors: he told mee he stopt for mee; and wee Rode on Very deliberatly a few paces, when we entred a Thickett of Trees and Shrubbs, and I perceived by the Hors's going we were on the descent of a Hill, w^{ch}, as wee come neerer the bottom, 'twas totaly dark wth the Trees that surrounded it. But I knew by the Going of the Hors wee had entred the water, wch my Guide told mee was the hazzardos River[1] he had told me off; and hee, Riding up close to my Side, Bid me not fear — we should be over Imediatly. I now ralyed all the Courage I was mistriss of, Knowing that I must either Venture my fate of drowning, or be left like ye Children in the wood. So, as the Post bid me, I gave Reins to my Nagg; and sitting as Stedy as Just before in the Cannoo, in a few minutes got safe to the other side, which hee told mee was the Narragansett country.[2]

[1] This is evidently Mascachuge river, a little south of East Greenwich. The road now by taking from the top of the hill and bridging filling up the hollow between the hills is very tolerable. But within the recollection of the writer the hills were very steep and it was a place dreaded by travelers and teamsters. A little farther south is Hunt's river, but the description does not at all agree with this. E. R. P.

[2] The Narragansett country, so called from the powerful tribe of that name who originally occupied it, lay between Narragansett bay and Pawcatuck river. It had been claimed both by Connecticut and by Rhode Island, and these claims had been for many years a cause of strife between those colonies. At one time it was formed into a nominally separate jurisdiction, under the name of The King's Province.

Here We found great difficulty in Travailing. the way being very narrow, and on each side the Trees and bushes gave us very unpleasent welcome wth their Branches and bow's, wch wee could not avoid, it being so exceeding dark. My Guide, as before so now, putt on harder than I, wth my weary bones, could follow; so left mee and the way behind him. Now Returned my distressed aprehensions of the place where I was: the dolesome woods, my Company next to none, Going I knew not whither, and encompased wth Terrifying darkness; The least of which was enough to startle a more Masculine courage. Added to which the Reflections, as in the afternoon of ye day that my Call was very Questionable, wch till then I had not so Prudently as I ought considered. Now, coming to ye foot of a hill, I found great difficulty in ascending; But being got to the Top, was there amply recompenced with the friendly Appearance of the Kind Conductress of the night, Just then Advancing above the Horisontall Line. The Raptures wch the Sight of that fair Planett produced in mee, caus'd mee, for the Moment, to forgett my present wearyness and past toils; and Inspir'd me for most of the remaining way with very divirting thot's, some of which, with the other Occurances of the day, I reserved to note down when I should come to my Stage. My tho'ts on the sight of the moon were to this purpose :

>Fair Cynthia, all the Homage that I may
>Unto a Creature, unto thee I pay;
>In Lonesome woods to meet so kind a guide,
>To Mee's more worth than all the world beside.
>Some Joy I felt just now, when safe got or'e
>Yon Surly River to this Rugged shore,
>Deeming Rough welcomes from these clownish Trees,
>Better than Lodgings wth Nereidees.
>Yet swelling fears surprise; all dark appears —
>Nothing but Light can disipate those fears.
>My fainting vitals can't lend strength to say,
>But softly whisper, O I wish 'twere day.
>The murmer hardly warm'd the Ambient air,
>E're thy Bright Aspect rescues from dispair:
>Makes the old Hagg her sable mantle loose,
>And a Bright Joy do's through my Soul diffuse.
>The Boistero's Trees now Lend a Passage Free,
>And pleasent prospects thou giv'st light to see.

From hence wee kept on, with more ease y^n

before: the way being smooth and even, the night warm and serene, and the Tall and thick Trees at a distance, especially w^n the moon glar'd light through the branches, fill'd my Imagination wth the pleasent delusion of a Sumpteous citty, fill'd wth famous Buildings and churches, wth their spiring steeples, Balconies, Galleries and I know not what: Granduers wch I had heard of, and wch the stories of foreign countries had given me the Idea of.

>Here stood a Lofty church—there is a steeple,
>And there the Grand Parade—O see the people!
>That Famouse Castle there, were I but nigh,
>To see the mote and Bridg and walls so high—
>They'r very fine! sais my deluded eye.

Being thus agreably entertain'd without a thou't of any thing but thoughts themselves, I on a suden was Rous'd from these pleasing Imaginations, by the Post's sounding his horn, which assured mee hee was arrived at the Stage, where we were to Lodg: and that musick was then most musickall and agreeable to mee.

Being come to mr. Havens',[1] I was very civilly

---

[1] Havens' Tavern, says Mr. Updike in his history of the Episco-

Received, and courteously entertained, in a clean comfortable House; and the Good woman was very active in helping off my Riding cloths, and then ask't what I would eat. I told her I had some Chocolett if shee would prepare it; which with the help of some Milk, and a little clean brass Kettle, she soon effected to my satisfaction. I then betook me to my Apartment, wch was a little Room parted from the Kitchen by a single bord partition; where, after I had noted the Occurrances of the past day, I went to bed, which, tho' pretty hard, Yet neet and handsome. But I could get no sleep, because of

pal church in Narragansett, stood on the site of the house of the late William P. Maxwell, Esq., in North Kingstown, a little south of the well known Devil's Foot rock.

It seems rather remarkable that Mrs. Knight does not mention this rock which is partly in the highway and was celebrated among the Indians. Its English name is a translation of the Indian name. (See *Records of North Kingston*, II, 54), and there were strange traditions of the devil's doings connected with it. A short distance south of Havens' was the residence of Lodowick Updike, one of the oldest and best known settlements in the country, settled before the great Indian war of 1675; Mr. Updike was then (1704) the proprietor of an immense estate and well known all over the state. (Potter's *Narragansett*, 270, 311, 166). It may perhaps be accounted for by her mode of traveling.   E. R. P.

the Clamor of some of the Town tope-ers in next Room, Who were entred into a strong debate concerning ye Signifycation of the name of their Country, (viz.) *Narraganset*. One said it was named so by ye Indians, because there grew a Brier there, of a prodigious Highth and bigness, the like hardly ever known, called by the Indians Narragansett; And quotes an Indian of so Barberous a name for his Author, that I could not write it. His Antagonist Replyed no — It was from a Spring it had its name, wch hee well knew where it was, which was extreem cold in summer, and as Hott as could be imagined in the winter, which was much resorted too by the natives, and by them called Narragánsett, (Hott and Cold,) and that was the originall of their places name—with a thousand Impertinances not worth notice, wch He utter'd with such a Roreing voice and Thundering blows with the fist of wickedness on the Table, that it peirced my very head. I heartily fretted, and wish't 'um tongue tyed; but wth as little succes as a freind of mine once, who was (as shee said) kept a whole night awake, on a Jorny, by a country Left, and a Sergent, Insigne and a Deacon, contriving how to bring a triangle into a Square. They kept calling for tother Gill, wch while they were swallowing, was some Intermission; But presently, like Oyle to fire, encreased the flame. I set my Candle on a Chest by the bed side, and setting up, fell to my old way of composing my Resentments, in the following manner:

I ask thy Aid, O Potent Rum!
To Charm these wrangling Topers Dum.
Thou hast their Giddy Brains possest—
The man confounded wth the Beast—
And I, poor I, can get no rest.
Intoxicate them with thy fumes:
O still their Tongues till morning comes.

And I know not but my wishes took effect; for the dispute soon ended w^th 'tother Dram; and so Good night!

Wednesday, Octob^r 4th. About four in the morning, we set off for Kingston[1] (for so was the Town called) with a french Docter[2] in our com-

[1] Properly Kingstown. It included the present towns of North Kingstown, South Kingstown and Exeter. Tower Hill was one of the earliest settlements and the one probably meant. E. R. P.

[2] A few miles west of the Havens tavern was a settlement of

pany. Hee and y⁰ Post put on very furiously, so that I could not keep up with them, only as now and then they'd stop till they see mee. This Rode was poorly furnished wth accommodations for Travellers, so that we were forced to ride 22 miles by the post's account, but neerer thirty by mine, before wee could bait so much as our Horses, wch I exceedingly complained of. But the post encourag'd mee, by saying wee should be well accommodated anon at mr. Devills,[1] a few miles further. But I questioned whether

French Huguenots. One of them, —— Ayrault, was a physician and probably the one mentioned by Mrs. Knight. (See Potter's *Narragansett*, 105, 109.   E. R. P.

[1] Davell's Mills, now Cross' Mills in Charlestown. Charlestown was formerly a part of the town of Westerly. (See Potter's *Narragansett*, 111, 226).

In going from Havens' to Davell's, Mrs. Knight passed, but probably before daylight, within a few rods of the Updike house before mentioned. As she crossed Tower hill, she was near the site of Bull's garrison house burnt in the previous Indian war. She then came in view of the sea and the famous Point Judith salt ponds. Near the present village of Wakefield she passed by the head of these ponds and directly by the side of Sugar Loaf hill, a hill which was known by that name in the time of Roger Williams. And farther on was a spring which before 1703 was known as Deadman's spring. A very short distance from Davell's, and near the road, stood an Indian fort well known we ought to go to the Devil[1] to be he'lpt out of affliction. However, like the rest of Deluded souls that post to ye Infernal denn, Wee made all posible speed to this Devil's Habitation; where alliting, in full assurance of good accommodation, wee were going in. But meeting his two daughters, as I suposed twins, they so neerly resembled each other, both in features and habit, and look't as old as the Divel himselfe, and quite as Ugly, We desired entertainm't, but could hardly get a word out of 'um, till with our Importunity, telling them our necesity, &c. they call'd the old Sophister, who was as sparing of his words as his daughters had bin, and no, or none, was the reply's hee made us to our demands. Hee differed only in this from the old fellow in to'ther Country : hee let us depart. However, I thought it proper to warn poor Travailers to endeavour to Avoid falling into cir-

in Indian history. Its remains are remarkable even at this day, and the place is called Fort Neck. These are not mentioned, probably because she was the only woman in the company and her mind was intent on the perils of her journey. E. R. P.

[1] This name of Davol or Davell was spelled Devil on old records of the time of Madam Knight. W. R. D.

cumstances like ours, wch at our next Stage I sat down and did as followeth:

> May all that dread the cruel feind of night
> Keep on, and not at this curs't Mansion light.
> 'Tis Hell; 'tis Hell! and Devills here do dwell:
> Here dwells the Devil—surely this's Hell.
> Nothing but Wants: a drop to cool yo'r Tongue
> Cant be procur'd these cruel Feinds among.
> Plenty of horrid Grins and looks sevear,
> Hunger and thirst, But pitty's bannish'd here—
> The Right hand keep, if Hell on Earth you fear!

Thus leaving this habitation of cruelty, we went forward; and arriving at an Ordinary[1] about two mile further, found tollerable accomodation. But our Hostes, being a pretty full mouth'd old creature, entertain'd our fellow travailer, ye french Doctor, wth Inumirable complaints of her bodily infirmities; and whisper'd to him so lou'd, that all ye House had as full a hearing as hee: which was very divirting to ye company, (of which there was a great many,)

[1] If the "Mr. Divel's" was at Davell's Mill, as we think, this ordinary might have been at the residence of the Champlins. This family settled there very early and were large proprietors; and in these days almost every house along the road afforded entertainment for travelers. E. R. P.

as one might see by their sneering. But poor weary I slipt out to enter my mind in my Jornal, and left my Great Landly with her Talkative Guests to themselves.

From hence we proceeded (about ten forenoon) through the Naragansett country, pretty Leisurely; and about one afternoon come to Paukataug River,[1] wch was about two hundred paces over, and now very high, and no way over to to'ther side but this. I darid not venture to Ride thro, my courage at best in such cases but small, And now at the Lowest Ebb, by reason of my weary, very weary, hungry and uneasy Circumstances. So takeing leave of my company, tho' wth no little Reluctance, that I could not proceed wth them on my Jorny, Stop at a little cottage Just by the River, to wait the Waters falling, wch the old man that lived there said would be in a little time, and he would conduct

[1] Mr. Updike informs me that Jesse Maxon, for many years Town clerk of Westerly who died a few years ago at an advanced age told him that the ancient riding over place at Westerly was five or six rods above the present bridge known as Pawcatuc Bridge. It was called Shaw's riding over place. A dwelling house now stands where the old way was.   E. R. P.

me safe over. This little Hutt was one of the wretchedest I ever saw a habitation for human creatures. It was suported with shores enclosed with Clapbords, laid on Lengthways, and so much asunder, that the Light come throu' every where; the doore tyed on wth a cord in ye place of hinges; The floor the bear earth; no windows but such as the thin covering afforded, nor any furniture but a Bedd wth a glass Bottle hanging at ye head on't; an earthan cupp, a small pewter Bason, A Bord wth sticks to stand on, instead of a table, and a block or two in ye corner instead of chairs. The family were the old man, his wife and two Children; all and every part being the picture of poverty. Notwithstanding both the Hutt and its Inhabitance were very clean and tydee: to the crossing the Old Proverb, that bare walls make giddy hows-wifes.

I Blest myselfe that I was not one of this misserable crew; and the Impressions their wretchedness formed in me caused mee on ye very Spott to say:

> Tho' Ill at ease, A stranger and alone,
> All my fatigu's shall not extort a grone.
> These Indigents have hunger with their ease;

Their best is wors behalfe than my disease.
Their Misirable hutt wch Heat and Cold
Alternately without Repulse do hold;
Their Lodgings thyn and hard, their Indian fare,
Their mean Apparel which the wretches wear,
And their ten thousand ills wch can't be told,
Makes nature er'e 'tis midle age'd look old.
When I reflect, my late fatigues do seem
Only a notion or forgotten Dreem.

I had scarce done thinking, when an Indian-like Animal come to the door, on a creature very much like himselfe, in mien and feature, as well as Ragged cloathing; and having 'litt, makes an Awkerd Scratch wth his Indian shoo, and a Nodd, sitts on ye block, fumbles out his black Junk, dipps it in ye Ashes, and presents it piping hott to his muscheeto's, and fell to sucking like a calf, without speaking, for near a quarter of an hower. At length the old man said how do's Sarah do? who I understood was the wretches wife and Daughter to ye old man: he Replyed—as well as can be expected, &c. So I remembred the old say, and suposed I knew Sarah's case. Butt hee being, as I understood, going over the River, as ugly as hee was, I was glad to ask him to show me y° way to Saxtons, at Stoningtown; wch he promising, I ventur'd over wth the old man's assistance; who having rewarded to content, with my Tattertailed guide, I Ridd on very slowly thro' Stoningtown, where the Rode was very Stony and uneven.[1] I asked the fellow, as we went, divers questions of the place and way, &c. I being arrived at my country Saxtons,[2] at Stonington, was very well accommodated both as to victuals and Lodging, the only Good of both I had found since my setting out. Here I heard there was an old man and his Daughter to come that way, bound to N. London; and being now destitute of a Guide, gladly waited for them, being in so good a harbour, and accordingly, Thirsday, Octob^r ye 5th, about 3 in the afternoon, I sat forward with

[1] After leaving Pawcatuck river, Madam Knight evidently took the old country road, leading over the hills through the central part of Stonington to the head of Mystic river.—Letter of Miss Caulkins, June 1865.

[2] Capt. Joseph Saxton, who died in 1715, lived some two or three miles east of Mystic. He is described in one document as formerly of Boston. "My Country" undoubtedly means "my countryman" and may indicate that they were both from Boston.—*Ibid.*

neighbour Polly[1] and Jemima, a Girl about 18 years old, who hee said he had been to fetch out of the Narragansetts, and said they had Rode thirty miles that day, on a sory lean jade, wth only a Bagg under her for a pillion, which the poor Girl often complain'd was very uneasy.

Wee made Good speed along wch made poor Jemima make many a sow'r face, the mare being a very hard trotter; and after many a hearty and bitter Oh, she at length Low'd out: Lawful Heart father! this bare mare hurts mee Dingeely, I'me direfull sore I vow; with many words to that purpose:—poor Child sais Gaffer—she us't to serve your mother so. I don't care how mother us't to do, quoth Jemima, in a passionate tone, at which the old man Laught, and kik't his Jade o' the side, which made her Jolt ten times harder.

About seven that Evening, we come to New London Ferry:[2] here, by reason of a very high

---

[1] This name appears in New London records.

[2] The ferry from Groton to New London had been leased to Cary Latham for fifty years from March 25th, 1655. The ferriage was 3d for a passenger, 6d for a horse or great beast and 3d for a calf or swine. In February 1701-2 the rent of the ferry, after

wind, we mett with great difficulty in getting over—the Boat tos't exceedingly, and our Horses capper'd at a very surprizing Rate, and sett us all in a fright; especially poor Jemima, who desired her father to say so jack to the Jade, to make her stand. But the careless parent, taking no notice of her repeated desires, She Rored out in a Passionate manner : Pray suth father, Are you deaf? Say so Jack to the Jade, I tell you. The Dutiful Parent obey's; saying so Jack, so Jack, as gravely as if hee'd bin to saying Catechise after Young Miss, who with her fright look't of all coullers in ye Rain Bow.

Being safely arrived at the house of. Mrs.

the expiration of this lease, was appropriated perpetually to the support of a public grammar school. The Parade, as it was called, lay at the foot of Court or State street in New London; and from the eastern part of the Parade the coast originally turned to the west, and was bordered by a strip of sand beach. At the head of this beach were the ferry stairs and the old town landing place, where in 1703 was built the town wharf. The railroad ferry by which travelers from Boston, by the way of Stonington, now cross on their way to New Haven and New York, lies farther south, even on the New London side. Down to 1800 the ferry boat was a scow, propelled by sails and oars. A rough passage, such as Madam Knight describes, was nothing unusual.— Miss Caulkins' *History of New London*, 80, 134, 180, 102.

Prentices[1] in N. London, I treated neighbour Polly and daughter for their divirting company, and bid them farewell; and between nine and ten at night waited on the Rev^d Mr. Gurdon Saltonstall,[2] minister of the town, who kindly Invited me to Stay that night at his house, where I was very handsomely and plentifully treated and Lodg'd; and made good the Great Character I had before heard concerning him:

[1] The old Prentis homestead was near the north end of Main street, where is now the old Deshon house. The first John Prentis died in 1691; and his relict, a third wife whom he had married late in life, survived him many years and kept a house of entertainment. More than one reference can be found to the tavern of the widow Prentis.— Miss Caulkins' letter.

[2] Gurdon Saltonstall, eldest son of Nathaniel Saltonstall of Haverhill, Mass., was born March 27, 1666; was graduated at Harvard where he was a distinguished scholar, and was ordained at New London in 1691. He became very celebrated as a preacher. On the death of Fitz John Winthrop in 1707, he was chosen governor of Connecticut; and he continued in that office till his death in 1724. "Who did not admire his consummate wisdom, profound learning, his dexterity in business and indefatigable application, his intimate acquaintance with men and things and his superior genius."— (*Funeral Discourse* by Rev. Eliphalet Adams.) Mr. Saltonstall's house was next to that of Mrs. Prentis, so that Madam Knight had not far to go in making her late evening visit.

viz. that he was the most affable, courteous Genero's and best of men.

Friday, Octo^r 6th. I got up very early, in Order to hire somebody to go with mee to New Haven, being in great parplexity at the thoughts of proceeding alone; which my most hospitable entertainer observing, himself went, and soon return'd wth a young Gentleman of the town, who he could confide in to Go with mee; and about eight this morning, wth Mr. Joshua Wheeler[1] my new Guide, takeing leave of this worthy Gentleman, Wee advanced on toward Seabrook. The Rodes all along this way are very bad, Incumbred wth Rocks and mountainos passages, wch were very disagreeable to my tired carcass; but we went on with a moderate pace wch made ye Journey more pleasent. But after about eight miles Rideing, in going over a Bridge[2] under

---

[1] Below the houses of Mr. Saltonstall and of Mrs. Prentis and on the opposite side of the way stood the Wheeler house. Mr. Saltonstall therefore *soon* returned. John Wheeler was one of the early shipping merchants of New London. His son Joshua, born in 1681, was undoubtedly Madam Knight's guide.— *Ibid.*

[2] This river must be the Niantic. At the crossing, known as Rope Ferry, there was no bridge until long after Madam Knight's

wch the River Run very swift, my hors stumbled, and very narrowly 'scaped falling over into the water; wch extreemly frightened mee. But through God's Goodness I met with no harm, and mounting agen, in about half a miles Rideing, come to an ordinary, were well entertained by a woman of about seventy and vantage, but of as Sound Intellectuals as one of seventeen. Shee entertain'd Mr. Wheeler wth some passages of a Wedding awhile ago at a place hard by, the Brides-Groom being about her Age or something above, Saying his Children was dredfully against their fathers marrying wch shee condemned them extreemly for.

From hence wee went pretty briskly forward, and arriv'd at Saybrook ferry about two of the day. She must therefore have crossed at the bridge near " River head;" which by the present road, is less than six miles from New London. This road is an old route, but may not have been opened as early as 1704. It is probable that Madam Knight went out on the old road that leads by Miss Latimer's, four miles; then turned west into the Douglas road, which at the end of two miles would bring her to a narrow, rugged road, (originally an old Indian trail,) that goes directly to the head of the river. She would thus have had her full eight miles of " *very bad Rodes Incumbred with Rocks and mountainos passages.*"— *Ibid.*

Clock afternoon; and crossing it, wee call'd at an Inn to Bait, (foreseeing we should not have such another Opportunity till we come to Killingsworth.) Landlady come in, with her hair about her ears, and hands at full pay scratching. Shee told us shee had some mutton wch shee would broil, wch I was glad to hear; But I supose forgot to wash her scratchers; in a little time shee brot it in; but it being pickled, and my Guide said it smelt strong of head sause, we left it, and p^d sixpence a piece for our Dinners, wch was only smell.

So wee putt forward with all speed, and about seven at night come to Killingsworth, and were tollerably well with Travillers fare, and Lodgd there that night.

Saturday, Oct. 7th, we sett out early in the Morning, and being something unaquainted wth the way, having ask't it of some wee mett, they told us wee must Ride a mile or two and turne down a Lane on the Right hand; and by their Direction wee Rode on, but not Yet comeing to ye turning, we mett a Young fellow and ask't him how farr it was to the Lane which turn'd down towards Guilford. Hee said wee must Ride a little further, and turn down by the Corner of uncle Sams Lott. My Guide vented his Spleen at the Lubber; and we soon after came into the Rhode, and keeping still on, without any thing further Remarkabell, about two a clock afternoon we arrived at New Haven, where I was received with all Posible Respects and civility. Here I discharged Mr. Wheeler with a reward to his satisfaction, and took some time to rest after so long and toilsome a Journey; And Inform'd myselfe of the manners and customs of the place, and at the same time employed myselfe in the afair I went there upon.

They are Govern'd by the same Laws as wee in Boston, (or little differing,) thr'out this whole Colony of Connecticot,[1] And much the same way of Church Government, and many of them good, Sociable people, and I hope Religious too: but a little too much Independant in their principalls,[2]

[1] "The earliest code in Connecticut, related only to capital offences. Adopted a year later than the Massachusetts Body of Liberties, it is in great part a verbal copy from that instrument." — Palfrey's *New England*, II, 31.

[2] "The habits of thought of this fraternity," (the settlers of

and, as I have been told, were formerly in their Zeal very Riggid in their Administrations towards such as their Lawes made Offenders, even to a harmless Kiss[1] or Innocent merriment among Young people. Whipping[2] being a frequent and counted an easy Punishment, about wch as other Crimes, the Judges were absolute[3] in their Sentances. They told mee a pleasant story about a pair of Justices in those parts, wch I may not omit the relation of.

New Haven,) " led them to carry out to its last results the idea which had fascinated so many thinking persons at that period, of finding in scripture a special rule for every thing of the nature of civil as well as of eccleasiastical order and administration."—Palfrey's *New England*, I, 528.

[1] The tradition of this strictness may have supplied a hint for one of the, so called, "Blue Laws:" "No woman shall kiss her child on the Sabbath or Fast day." And at least it is evident from this Journal that the story of some New Haven legislation against kissing had existed long before 1781 when Samuel Peters published his history of Connecticut, in which, (as it is said,) the fiction of the "Blue Laws" first appeared.—Kingsley's *Historical Discourse*, 84.

[2] "Defamation had in some instances been punished by fine, repeated scourgings and imprisonment."—Trumbull's *History of Connecticut*, I, 177.

[3] This probably refers to the absence in earlier times of the trial by Jury and the want of any body of statutes; the Mosaic

A negro Slave belonging to a man in ye Town, stole a hogs head from his master, and gave or sold it to an Indian, native of the place. The Indian sold it in the neighbourhood, and so the theft was found out. Thereupon the Heathen was Seized, and carried to the Justices House to be Examined. But his worship (it seems) was gone into the feild, with a Brother in office, to gather in his Pompions. Whither the malefactor is hurried, And Complaint made, and satisfaction in the name of Justice demanded. Their Worships cann't proceed in form without a Bench: whereupon they Order one to be Imediately erected, which, for want of fitter materials, they made with pompions — which being finished, down setts their Worships, and the Malefactor call'd, and by the Senior Justice Interrogated after the following manner. You Indian why did You steal from this man? You sho'dn't do so — it's a Grandy wicked thing to steal. Hol't Hol't cryes Justice Junr Brother, You speak

law being established as the rule to all courts, until it should be "branched out into particulars." "Until this time punishments in many instances had been uncertain and arbitrary. They had been left wholly to the discretion of the court."—Trumbull, I, 177.

negro to him. I'le ask him. You sirrah, why did You steal this man's Hoggshead? Hoggshead, (replys the Indian,) me no stomany.¹ No? says his Worship; and pulling off his hatt, Patted his own head with his hand, sais, Tatapa²—You, Tatapa—you; all one this. Hoggshead all one this. Hah! says Netop,³ now me stomany that. Whereupon the Company fell into a great fitt of Laughter, even to Roreing. Silence is comanded, but to no effect: for they continued perfectly Shouting. Nay, sais his worship, in an angry tone, if it be so, *take mee off the Bench.*

Their Diversions in this part of the Country are on Lecture days and Training days mostly: on the former there is Riding from town to town.

And on training dayes The Youth divert themselves by Shooting at the Target, as they call it, (but it very much resembles a pillory,)

¹ *Query :* Corruption of *understand.*

² *Tatta pitch* is said to mean: I cannot tell.— Roger Williams Key, *Mass. Historical Collections,* 1st series, v, 89.

³ "What cheer Netop, is the general salutation of all English to them. *Netop* is friend."—Roger Williams Key, *Mass. Historical Collections,* 1st series, III, 207.

where hee that hitts neerest the white has some yards of Red Ribbin presented him, wch being tied to his hattband, the two ends streeming down his back, he is Led away in Triumph, wth great applause, as the winners of the Olympiack Games. They generally marry very young: the males oftener as I am told under twentie than above; they generally make public wedings, and have a way something singular (as they say) in some of them, viz. Just before Joyning hands the Bridegroom quitts the place, who is soon followed by the Bridesmen, and as it were, dragg'd back to duty—being the reverse to ye former practice among us, to steal m^s Pride.

There are great plenty of Oysters all along by the sea side, as farr as I Rode in the Collony, and those very good. And they Generally lived very well and comfortably in their famelies. But too Indulgent (especially ye farmers) to their slaves: sufering too great familiarity from them, permitting y^m to sit at Table and eat with them, (as they say to save time,) and into the dish goes the black hoof as freely as the white hand. They told me that there was a farmer lived nere the Town where I lodgd who had some difference wth his slave, concerning something the master had promised him and did not punctualy perform; wch caused some hard words between them; But at length they put the matter to Arbitration and Bound themselves to stand to the award of such as they named — wch done, the Arbitrators Having heard the Allegations of both parties, Order the master to pay 40^s to black face, and acknowledge his fault. And so the matter ended : the poor master very honestly standing to the award.[1]

There are every where in the Towns as I passed, a Number of Indians the Natives of the Country, and are the most salvage of all the salvages of that kind that I had ever Seen : little or no care taken (as I heard upon enquiry) to make them otherwise. They have in some places Landes of theire owne, and Govern'd by Law's of their own making ;— they marry many wives and at pleasure put them away, and on the ye least dislike or fickle humor, on either

---

[1] From this little incident it may be seen that, even at this early time, slavery, in Connecticut, was a very different thing from the system which has existed in the southern part of our country.

side, saying *stand away* to one another is a sufficient Divorce. And indeed those uncomely *Stand aways* are too much in Vougue among the English in this (Indulgent Colony) as their Records plentifully prove, and that on very trivial matters, of which some have been told me, but are not proper to be Related by a Female pen, tho some of that foolish sex have had too large a share in the story.[1]

If the natives committ any crime on their own precints among themselves, ye English takes no Cognezens of. But if on the English

[1] This facility for obtaining divorce may have arisen from the degradation of marriage to a mere civil contract entered into before a magistrate. It was certainly in striking contrast with the strictness which could lead a grand jury to present a young man and woman "for sitting together on the Lord's day under an apple tree." Unfortunately the same facility has continued to the present time in this "indulgent colony." Courts can divorce for a desertion of three years, for habitual drunkenness and for such *misconduct as permanently destroys the hpppiness of the other party and defeats the purposes of the marriage relation!* While a standing committee of every legislature was until recently at the service of such persons as could not meet even the easy requirements for judicial relief. And these divorces were all *a vinculo*. The present governor of that state officially speaks of these practices as: "a scandal upon our reputation and a reproach to our morals and our religion."

ground, they are punishable by our Laws. They mourn for their Dead by blacking their faces, and cutting their hair, after an Awkerd and frightfull manner; But can't bear You should mention the names of their dead Relations to them: they trade most for Rum, for wch they^d hazzard their very lives; and the English fit them Generally as well, by seasoning it plentifully with water.

They give the title of merchant to every trader; who Rate their Goods according to the time and spetia they pay in: viz. Pay, mony, Pay as mony, and trusting. *Pay* is Grain, Pork, Beef, &c. at the prices sett by the General Court that Year;[1] *mony* is pieces of Eight, Ryalls, or Boston or Bay shillings (as they call them,) or Good hard money, as sometimes silver coin is termed by them; also Wampom, vizt Indian beads wch serves for change. *Pay as mony* is provisions, as afores^d one Third cheaper then

[1] In laying taxes, or rates, the general court often provided that they might be paid in wheat or certain other agricultural products, at specified prices. For instances see *Connecticut Public Records* (1655-77) 269, 322.

as the Assembly or Gene^l Court setts it; and *Trust* as they and the merch^t agree for time.

Now, when the buyer comes to ask for a comodity, sometimes before the merchant answers that he has it, he sais, *is Your pay redy?* Perhaps the Chap Reply's Yes: what do You pay in? say's the merchant. The buyer having answered, then the price is set; as suppose he wants a sixpenny knife, in pay it is 12d — in pay as money eight pence, and hard money its own price, viz. 6d. It seems a very Intricate way of trade and what Lex Mercatoria had not thought of.

Being at a merchants house, in comes a tall country fellow wth his alfogeos¹ full of Tobacco; for they seldom Loose their Cudd, but keep Chewing and Spitting as long as they'r eyes are open — he advanc't to the midle of the Room, makes an Awkward Nodd, and spitting a Large deal of Aromatick Tincture, he gave a scrape with his shovel like shoo, leaving a small shovel

¹ This word is probably a corruption of the Spanish *alfoja*, saddlebag, portmanteau, or of the Portuguese *alforges* (plural), a wallet or bag, usually for provisions; and it here seems to mean a tobacco pouch.

full of dirt on the floor, made a full stop, Hugging his own pretty Body with his hands under his arms, Stood staring rown'd him, like a Catt let out of a Baskett. At last, like the creature Balaam Rode on, he opened his mouth and said: have You any Ribinen for Hatbands to sell I pray? The Questions and Answers about the pay being past, the Ribin is bro't and opened. Bumpkin Simpers, cryes its confounded Gay I vow; and beckning to the door, in comes Jone Tawdry, dropping about 50 curtsees, and stands by him: hee shows her the Ribin. *Law You,* sais shee, *its right Gent,* do You take it, *tis dreadfull pretty.* Then she enquires, *have You any hood silk I pray?* wch being brought and bought, Have You any *thred silk to sew it wth* says shee, wch being accomodated wth they Departed. They Generaly stand after they come in a great while speachless, and sometimes dont say a word till they are askt what they want, which I Impute to the Awe they stand in of the merchants, who they are constantly almost Indebted too; and must take what they bring without Liberty to choose for themselves; but they serve them as well, making the merchants stay long enough for their pay.

We may Observe here the great necessity and bennifitt both of Education and Conversation; for these people have as Large a portion of mother witt, and sometimes a Larger, than those who have bin brought up in Citties; But for want of emprovements, Render themselves almost Ridiculos, as above.[1] I should be glad if they would leave such follies, and am sure all that Love Clean Houses (at least) would be glad on't too.

They are generaly very plain in their dress, throuout all ye Colony, as I saw, and follow one another in their modes; that You may know where they belong, especially the women, meet them where you will.

Their Cheif Red Letter day is St. Election,[2] wch is annualy Observed according to Charter, to choose their Goven^r: a blessing they can

[1] From the tone of this sentiment one might think that Madam Knight had already commenced her school keeping.

[2] "It was first the custom and afterwards the order that the ministers of the gospel should preach a sermon on the day appointed for the choice of civil rulers."— Bancroft's *Hist* III, 69.

never be thankfull enough for, as they will find if ever it be their hard fortune to loose it.[1] The present Govenor in Conecticott is the Honble John Winthrop, Esq.[2] A Gentleman of an Ancient and Honourable Family, whose Father[3] was Govenor here sometime before, and his Grand father had bin Govr of the Massachusetts. This gentleman is a very curteous and afable person, much Given to Hospitality, and has by his Good services Gain'd the affections of the people as much as any who had bin before him in that post.

Decr 6th. Being by this time well Recruited and rested after my Journy, my business lying

[1] The allusion here is to the proceedings on the part of Lord Cornbury and Gov. Dudley to take away the Connecticut charter; in which they were favored by the difficulties arising out of the Liveen will.—Bancroft's *Hist*. III, 70. Trumbull's *Hist*. I, 417. Miss Caulkins' *New London*, chap. xv.

[2] Major General Fitz-John Winthrop was elected Governor of Connecticut in 1698. He was born in 1638, and died at Boston in 1707. He had been the Commander-in-chief of the unfortunate expedition against Canada in 1690. Perhaps the ill-will felt towards him in New York on account of that failure increased his popularity in Connecticut.

[3] John Winthrop "the younger."

unfinished by some concerns at New York depending thereupon, my Kinsman, Mr. Thomas Trowbridge[1] of New Haven, must needs take a Journy there before it could be accomplished, I resolved to go there in company wth him, and a man of the town wch I engaged to wait on me there. Accordingly, Dec. 6th we set out from New Haven, and about 11 same morning came to Stratford ferry[2]; wch crossing, about two miles on the other side Baited our horses and would have eat a morsell ourselves, But the Pumpkin and Indian mixt Bred[3] had such an Aspect, and the Bare-legg'd Punch so awkerd or rather Awfull a sound, that we left both, and proceeded forward, and about seven at night come to Fairfield, where we met with good entertainment and Lodg'd; and early next morning set forward to Norowalk,[4] from its halfe Indian name *North-walk*, when about 12 at noon

[1] Thomas Trowbridge, son of Thomas and of Sarah Rutherford, his wife, born Feb. 14, 1664. Savage's *Genealogical Dictionary*.

[2] See *Conn. Public Records* (1655-77) 136, 253.

[3] Bread made of Indian meal with a mixture of pumpkin.

[4] Narawauk, now Norwalk, has the same origin and meaning with Norridgewock; from *nara*, still water below falls, *wampi* clear, *ack*, locative. — *Historical Magazine*, IX, 91.

we arrived, and Had a Dinner of Fryed Venison, very savoury. Landlady wanting some pepper in the seasoning, bid the Girl hand her the spice in the little *Gay* cupp on ye shelfe. From hence we Hasted towards Rye, walking and Leading our Horses neer a mile together, up a prodigios high Hill; and so Riding till about nine at night, and there arrived and took up our Lodgings at an ordinary, wch a French family kept. Here being very hungry, I desired a fricasee wch the Frenchman undertakeing, managed so contrary to my notion of Cookery, that I hastned to Bed superless; And being shewd the way up a pair of stairs wch had such a narrow passage that I had almost stopt by the Bulk of my Body, But arriving at my apartment found it to be a little Lento Chamber furnisht amongst other Rubbish with a High Bedd and a Low one, a Long Table, a Bench and a Bottomless chair,— Little Miss went to scratch up my Kennell wch Russelled as if shee'd bin in the Barn amongst the Husks, and supose such was the contents of the tickin — nevertheless being exceeding weary, down I laid my poor Carkes (never more tired) and found my Covering as scanty as my Bed was hard. Annon I heard another Russelling noise in Y^e Room — called to know the matter — Little miss said shee was making a bed for the men; who, when they were in Bed, complained their leggs lay out of it by reason of its shortness — my poor bones complained bitterly not being used to such Lodgings, and so did the man who was with us; and poor I made but one Grone, which was from the time I went to bed to the time I Riss, which was about three in the morning, Setting up by the Fire till Light, and having discharged our ordinary wch was as dear as if we had had far Better fare — we took our leave of Monsier and about seven in the morn come to New Rochell a french town, where we had a good Breakfast. And in the strength of that about an how'r before sunsett got to York. Here I applyd myself to Mr. Burroughs,[1] a merchant to whom I was recommended by my Kinsman Capt. Prout, and received great Civil-

---

[1] Probably Thomas Burroughs, a prominent Merchant. Valentine's *History of New York*, 219. In a census taken in 1703 his name appears as a resident of Dock Ward. *Documentary History of N. Y.*, I, 611. He was a vestryman of Trinity church.

ities from him and his spouse, who were now
both Deaf but very agreeable in their Conversation, Diverting me with pleasant stories of their
knowledge in Brittan from whence they both
come, one of which was above the rest very
pleasant to me viz. my Lord Darcy had a very
extravagant Brother who had mortgaged what
Estate hee could not sell, and in good time dyed
leaving only one son. Him his Lordship (having none of his own) took and made him Heir
of his whole Estate, which he was to receive at
the death of his Aunt. He and his Aunt in her
widowhood held a right understanding and lived
as become such Relations, shee being a discreat
Gentlewoman and he an Ingenios Young man.
One day Hee fell into some Company though far
his inferiors, very freely told him of the Ill circumstances his fathers Estate lay under, and the
many Debts he left unpaid to the wrong of poor
people with whom he had dealt. The Young
gentleman was put out of countenance — no way
hee could think of to Redress himself — his
whole dependance being on the Lady his Aunt,
and how to speak to her he knew not — Hee

went home, sat down to dinner and as usual sometimes with her when the Chaplain was absent, she desired him to say Grace, wch he did after this manner:

> Pray God in Mercy take my Lady Darcy
> Unto his Heavenly Throne,
> That Little John may live like a man,
> And pay every man his own.

The prudent Lady took no present notice, But finishd dinner, after wch having sat and talk't awhile (as Customary) He Riss, took his Hatt and Going out she desired him to give her leave to speak to him in her Clossett, Where being come she desired to know why hee prayed for her Death in the manner aforesaid, and what part of her deportment towards him merritted such desires. Hee Reply'd, none at all, But he was under such disadvantages that nothing but that could do him service, and told her how he had been affronted as above, and what Impressions it had made upon him. The Lady made him a gentle reprimand that he had not informed her after another manner, Bid him see what his father owed and he should have money to pay it to a penny, And always to lett her know his wants and he should have a redy supply. The Young Gentleman charm'd with his Aunts Discrete management, Beggd her pardon and accepted her kind offer and retrieved his fathers Estate, &c. and said Hee hoped his Aunt would never dye, for shee had done better by him than hee could have done for himself.—Mr. Burroughs went with me to Vendue where I bought about 100 Rheem of paper wch was retaken in a flyboat from Holland and sold very Reasonably here— some ten, some Eight shillings per Rheem by the Lott wch was ten Rheem in a Lott. And at the Vendue I made a great many acquaintances amongst the good women of the town, who curteosly invited me to their houses and generously entertained me.

The Cittie of New York is a pleasant well compacted place, situated on a Commodius River wch is a fine harbour for shipping. The Buildings Brick Generaly, very stately and high, though not altogether like ours in Boston. The Bricks in some of the Houses are of divers Coullers and laid in Checkers, being glazed look very agreeable. The inside of them are neat to admiration, the wooden work, for only the walls are plasterd, and the Sumers and Gist[1] are plained and kept very white scowr'd as so is all the partitions if made of Bords. The fire places have no Jambs (as ours have) But the Backs run flush with the walls, and the Hearth is of Tyles and is as farr out into the Room at the Ends as before the fire, wch is Generally Five foot in the Low'r rooms, and the peice over where the mantle tree should be is made as ours with Joyners work, and as I supose is fasten'd to iron rodds inside. The House where the Vendue was, had Chimney Corners like ours, and they and the hearths were laid wth the finest tile that I ever see, and the stair cases laid all with white tile which is ever clean,[2] and so are

[1] Summers and joist. The summer, a word not now in very common use, was a central beam supporting the joist; such as is now sometimes called the *bearing-beam*.

[2] The tiles were set into the wall; forming, as it were, a continuous border, or row, of the width of one tile (or perhaps sometimes of more), close to the upper line of the staircase.

The Coeymans house, standing on the bank of the Hudson, just north of the village of Coeymans, still shows most of these peculiarities of building mentioned by Madam Knight:— the

the walls of the Kitchen wch had a Brick floor. They were making Great preparations to Receive their Govenor, Lord Cornbury from the Jerseys, and for that End raised the militia to Gard him on shore to the fort.[1]

They are Generaly of the Church of England and have a New England Gentleman[2] for their minister, and a very fine church set out with all Customary requsites. There are also a Dutch[3] and Divers Conventicles as they call them, viz.

staircase laid with tiles; no plaster except on the walls; and heavy floor-timbers, strengthened at the ends by solid knees, planed and "kept very white scoured."

[1] On the block between Bowling Green, Whitehall, Bridge and State streets. — Valentine's *History of New York*, 28.

[2] William Vesey, previously "a dissenting preacher on Long Island. He had received his education in Harvard under that rigid Independent, Increase Mather, and was sent from thence by him to confirm the minds of those who had removed for their convenience from New England to this Province. * * * But Col. Fletcher, who saw into his design, took off Mr. Vesey by an invitation to this Living; * * * and Mr. Vesey returned from England in Priest's orders." — *Documentary History of New York*, III, 438.

[3] The Reformed Dutch Church built in 1693 in what is now Exchange Place. — Greenleaf's *History of N. Y. Churches*. 11.

Baptist,[1] Quakers,[2] &c. They are not strict in keeping the Sabbath as in Boston and other places where I had bin, But seem to deal with great exactness as farr as I see or Deall with. They are sociable to one another and Curteos and Civill to strangers and fare well in their houses. The English go very fasheonable in their dress. Dut the Dutch, especially the middling sort, differ from our women, in their habitt go loose, were French muches wch are like a Capp and a head band in one, leaving their ears bare, which are sett out wth Jewells of a large size and many in number. And their fingers hoop't with Rings, some with large stones in them of many Coullers as were their pendants in their ears, which You should see very old women wear as well as Young.

They have Vendues very frequently and

[1] Greenleaf however gives 1799 as the first Baptist preaching; that of Wickenden. A petition of Nicholas Eyres states that in 1715 his house was registered for an anabaptist meeting house. — *D,cumentary History of New York*, III, 480.

[2] The first Friends' Meeting House, a small frame building, standing on Little Green Street, is said to have been erected in 1696 or 1703. — *Greenleaf*, 116.

make their Earnings very well by them, for they treat with good Liquor Liberally, and the Customers Drink as Liberally and Generally pay for't as well, by paying for that which they Bidd up Briskly for, after the sack has gone plentifully about, tho' sometimes good penny worths are got there. Their Diversions in the Winter is Riding Sleys about three or four Miles out of Town, where they have Houses of entertainment at a place called the Bowery,[1] and some go to friends Houses who handsomely treat them. Mr. Burroughs carry'd his spouse and Daughter and myself out to one Madame Dowes, a Gentlewoman that lived at a farm House, who gave us a handsome Entertainment of five or six Dishes and choice Beer and metheglin, Cyder, &c. all which she said was the produce of her farm. I believe we mett 50 or 60 slays that day — they fly with great swiftness and some are so furious that they'le turn out of the path

[1] "A small tavern stood on the banks of the Harlem river. This tavern was the occasional point of excursion for riding parties from the City and was known as the 'Wedding Place.' One or two small taverns were on the road between the town and the Bowery." — Valentine's *History of New York*, 69.

for none except a Loaden Cart. Nor do they spare for any diversion the place affords, and sociable to a degree, they'r Tables being as free to their Naybours as to themselves.

Having here transacted the affair I went upon and some other that fell in the way, after about a fortnight's stay there I left New York with no Little regrett, and Thursday, Dec. 21, set out for New Haven wth my Kinsman Trowbridge, and the man that waited on me about one afternoon, and about three come to half-way house about ten miles out of town, where we Baited and went forward, and about 5 come to Spiting Devil, Else Kings bridge, where they pay three pence for passing over with a horse, which the man that keeps the Gate set up at the end of the Bridge receives.

We hoped to reach the french town and Lodg there that night, but unhapily lost our way about four miles short, and being overtaken by a great storm of wind and snow which set full in our faces about dark, we were very uneasy. But meeting one Gardner who lived in a Cottage thereabout, offered us his fire to set by, having but one poor Bedd, and his wife not well, &c. or he would go to a House with us, where he thought we might be better accommodated —thither we went, But a surly old shee Creature, not worthy the name of woman, who would hardly let us go into her Door, though the weather was so stormy none but shee would have turnd out a Dogg. But her son whose name was gallop, who lived Just by Invited us to his house and shewed me two pair of stairs, viz. one up the loft and tother up the Bedd, wch was as hard as it was high, and warmed it with a hott stone at the feet. I lay very uncomfortably, insomuch that I was so very cold and sick I was forced to call them up to give me something to warm me. They had nothing but milk in the house, wch they Boild, and to make it better sweetened wth molasses, which I not knowing or thinking oft till it was down and coming up agen wch it did in so plentifull a manner that my host was soon paid double for his portion, and that in specia. But I believe it did me service in Cleering my stomach. So after this sick and weary night at East Chester, (a very miserable poor place,) the weather being now fair, Friday the 22^d Dec. we set out for New Rochell, where being come we had good Entertainment and Recruited ourselves very well. This is a very pretty place well compact, and good handsome houses, Clean, good and passable Rodes, and situated on a Navigable River, abundance of land well fined and Cleerd all along as wee passed, which caused in me a Love to the place, wch I could have been content to live in it. Here wee Ridd over a Bridge made of one entire stone of such a Breadth that a cart might pass with safety, and to spare — it lay over a passage cutt through a Rock to convey water to a mill not farr off. Here are three fine Taverns within call of each other, very good provision for Travailers.

Thence we travailed through Merrinak,[1] a neet, though little place, wth a navigable River before it, one of the pleasantest I ever see — Here were good Buildings, Especialy one, a very fine seat, wch they told me was Col. Heth-

[1] Mamaroneck.

coats,[1] who I had heard was a very fine Gentleman. From hence we come to Hors Neck,[2] where wee Baited, and they told me that one Church of England parson officiated in all these three towns once every Sunday in turns throughout the Year; and that they all could but poorly maintaine him, which they grudg'd to do, being a poor and quarelsome crew as I understand by our Host; their Quarelling about their choice of Minister, they chose to have none—But caused the Government to send this Gentleman to them. Here wee took leave of York Government, and Descending the Mountainos passage that almost broke my heart in ascending before, we come to Stamford, a well compact Town, but miserable meeting house, wch we passed, and thro' many and great difficulties, as Bridges which were exceeding high and very tottering and of vast Length, steep and Rocky Hills and precipices, (Buggbears to a fearful female travailer.) About nine at night we come to Norr-

[1] Col. Caleb Heathcote, of Scarsdale Manor. See *Colonial History of New York; passim.*
[2] West Greenwich.

walk, having crept over a timber of a Broken Bridge[1] about thirty foot long, and perhaps fifty to ye water. I was exceeding tired and cold when we come to our Inn, and could get nothing there but poor entertainment, and the Impertinant Bable of one of the worst of men, among many others of which our Host made one, who, had he bin one degree Impudenter, would have outdone his Grandfather. And this I think is the most perplexed night I have yet had. From hence, Saturday, Dec. 23, a very cold and windy day, after an Intolerable night's Lodging, wee hasted forward only observing in our way the Town to be situated on a Navigable river wth indiferent Buildings and people more refind than in some of the Country towns wee had passed, tho' vicious enough, the Church and Tavern being next neighbours. Having Ridd thro a difficult River[2] wee come to Fairfield

[1] A committee was appointed by the town of Norwalk February, 20, 1694-5 to "take an exact view of the Bridge over Norwalk River and to repaire the same, *eyther by erecting a new bridge*, or by repairing the old." — Hall's *Norwalk Records*, 88.

[2] Probably the Saugatuck.

where wee Baited and were much refreshed as well with the Good things wch gratified our appetites as the time took to rest our wearied Limbs, wch Latter I employed in enquiring concerning the Town and manners of the people, &c. This is a considerable town, and filld as they say with wealthy people — have a spacious meeting house and good Buildings. But the Inhabitants are Litigious, nor do they well agree with their minister, who (they say) is a very worthy Gentleman.[1]

They have aboundance of sheep, whose very Dung brings them great gain, with part of which they pay their Parsons sallery, And they Grudg that, prefering their Dung before their minister. They Lett out their sheep at so much as they agree upon for a night; the highest Bidder always caries them, And they will sufficiently Dung a Large quantity of Land before morning.

[1] Joseph Webb, ordained at Fairfield in 1694. Even before his time the General Court appointed a committee "to improve there best abillities to settle an accomadation between the people and minister of Fayrefeild, that so if it be the will of God Mr. Wakeman may continue in his worke there."—*Conn. Public Records*, 240.

But were once Bitt by a sharper who had them a night and sheared them all before morning — From hence we went to Stratford, the next Town, in which I observed but few houses, and those not very good ones. But the people that I conversed with were civill and good natured. Here we staid till late at night, being to cross a Dangerous River ferry, the River[1] at that time full of Ice; but after about four hours waiting with great difficulty wee got over. My fears and fatigues prevented my here taking any particular observation. Being got to Milford, it being late in the night, I could go no further; my fellow travailer going forward, I was invited to Lodg at Mrs. ——, a very kind and civill Gentlewoman, by whom I was handsomely and kindly entertained till the next night. The people here go very plain in their apparel (more plain than I had observed in the towns I had passed) and seem to be very grave and serious. They told me there was a singing Quaker[2] lived

[1] The Housatonic.

[2] " One Case and one Banks, two lewd men called *singing Quakers*, coming through the Colony, singing and dancing, accompa-

there, or at least had a strong inclination to be so, His Spouse not at all affected that way. Some of the singing Crew come there one day to visit him, who being then abroad, they sat down (to the woman's no small vexation) Humming and singing and groneing after their conjuring way—Says the woman are you singing quakers? Yea says They—Then take my squalling Brat of a child here and sing to it says she for I have almost split my throat wth singing to him and cant get the Rogue to sleep. They took this as a great Indignity, and mediately departed. Shaking the dust from their Heels left the good woman and her Child among the number of the wicked.

This is a Seaport place and accomodated with a Good Harbour, But I had not opportunity to make particular observations because it was Sabbath day—This Evening.[1]

nied with a number of women to assist them in their musical exercises and especially to proclaim how their lips dropped with myrrh and honey."—Trumbull's *Hist. Conn.*, II, 36, note.

[1] It was Saturday; and, according to the well known Connecticut custom, the "Sabbath" commenced at "sundown" on Saturday.

December 24.[1] I set out with the Gentlewomans son who she very civilly offered to go with me when she see no parswasions would cause me to stay which she pressingly desired, and crossing a ferry having but nine miles to New Haven, in a short time arrived there and was Kindly received and well accommodated amongst my Friends and Relations.

The Government of Connecticut Collony begins westward towards York at Stanford[2] (as I am told) and so runs Eastward towards Boston (I mean in my range, because I dont intend to extend my description beyond my own travails) and ends that way at Stonington—And has a great many Large towns lying more northerly. It is a plentiful Country for provisions of all sorts and its Generally Healthy. No one that can and will be dilligent in this place need fear poverty nor the want of food and Rayment.

[1] Madam Knight states that, arriving at Milford, she was entertained till the next night. Probably therefore it was on Monday, the 25th of December, that she went on to New Haven, and the date in the journal is erroneous.

[2] See account of the arbitration in 1650, as to the boundary line.—Palfrey's *New England*, II, 311.

January 6th. Being now well Recruited and fitt for business I discoursed the persons I was concerned with, that we might finnish in order to my return to Boston. They delay^d as they had hitherto done hoping to tire my Patience. But I was resolute to stay and see an End of the matter let it be never so much to my disadvantage —So January 9th they come again and promise the Wednesday following to go through with the distribution of the Estate which they delayed till Thursday and then come with new amusements. But at length by the mediation of that holy good Gentleman, the Rev. Mr. James Pierpont,[1] the minister of New Haven, and with the advice and assistance of other our Good friends we come to an accommodation and distribution, which having finished though not till February, the man that waited on me to

[1] Rev. James Pierpont was graduated at Harvard, and in 1685 was ordained at New Haven. He died there in 1714. "In the pulpit Mr. Pierpont was distinguished among his cotemporaries. His personal appearance was altogether prepossessing. He was eminent in the gift of prayer. His doctrine was sound and discriminating and his style was clear, lively and impressive."— Baron's *Historical Discourses*.

York taking the charge of me I sit out for Boston. We went from New Haven upon the ice (the ferry being not passable thereby) and the Rev. Mr. Pierpont wth Madam Prout[1] Cuzin Trowbridge and divers others were taking leave wee went onward without any thing Remarkabl till wee come to New London and Lodged again at Mr. Saltonstalls — and here I dismist my Guide, and my Generos entertainer provided me Mr. Samuel Rogers[2] of that place to go home with me — I stayed a day here Longer than I intended by the Commands of the Hon[ble] Govenor Winthrop to stay and take a supper with him whose wonderful civility I may not omitt.

[1] John Prout of New Haven, son of Timothy Prout of Boston, married, August 23, 1681, Mary, widow of Daniel Hall and daughter of Henry Rutherford. Sarah, another daughter, was the wife of Thomas Trowbridge, who died in 1702, and who was the father of the Thomas Trowbridge mentioned by Madam Knight. Savage's *Geneal. Dictionary.* It is possible therefore that Madam Knight's relationship with the Prout and Trowbridge families was through the Rutherfords.

[2] There were many of this family name at New London. One, possibly a brother of Madam Knight's companion, was the founder of a strange religious sect, of local notoriety; the Rogerenes.

The next morning I Crossed ye Ferry to Groton, having had the Honor of the Company, of Madam Livingston[1] (who is the Govenors Daughter) and Mary Christophers[2] and divers others to the boat—And that night Lodg^d at Stonington and had Rost Beef and pumpkin sause for supper. The next night at Haven's and had Rost fowle, and the next day wee come to a river which by Reason of Y^e Freshetts coming down was swell'^{d} so high wee fear^d it impassable and the rapid stream was very terryfying—However we must over and that in a small Canoo. Mr. Rogers assuring me of his good Conduct, I after a stay

[1] Mary, the only child of Fitz-John Winthrop, the Governor of Connecticut, was the wife of Lieut. Col. John Livingston. She died at Uncasville a few miles north of New London, January 8th, 1712-13. She was not buried until the 16th, on account of the inclemency of the weather and the depth of the snow. A few months after her death, Col. Livingston married Elizabeth, the only child of Madam Knight, mentioned on a following page.

Col. Livingston came from New York to Connecticut after the failure of the expedition to Canada in 1690, sharing the blame which was thrown on Gen. Winthrop. He resided in New London till 1718, and then went to England where he died.

[2] Probably the daughter of Christopher Christophers. The family of this name was large and influential in New London and was connected with Madam Knight by marriage.

of near an how'r on the shore for consultation went into the Canoo, and Mr. Rogers paddled about 100 yards up the Creek by the shore side, turned into the swift stream and dexterously steering her in a moment wee come to the other side as swiftly passing as an arrow shott out of the Bow by a strong arm. I staid on ye shore till Hee returned to fetch our horses, which he caused to swim over himself bringing the furniture in the Cannoo. But it is past my skill to express the Exceeding fright all their transactions formed in me. Wee were now in the colony of the Massachusetts and taking Lodgings at the first Inn we come too had a pretty difficult passage the next day which was the second of March by reason of the sloughy ways then thawed by the Sunn. Here I mett Capt. John Richards of Boston who was going home, So being very glad of his Company we Rode something harder than hitherto, and missing my way in going up a very steep Hill, my horse dropt down under me as Dead ; this new surprize no little hurt me meeting it Just at the Entrance into Dedham from whence we intended to reach home that night. But was now obliged to gett another Hors there and leave my own, resolving for Boston that night if possible. But in going over the Causeway at Dedham the Bridge being overflowed by the high waters comming down I very narrowly escaped falling over into the river Hors and all wch twas almost a miracle I did not—now it grew late in the afternoon and the people having very much discouraged us about the sloughy way wch they said wee should find very difficult and hazardous it so wrought on mee being tired and dispirited and disapointed of my desires of going home that I agreed to Lodg there that night wch wee did at the house of one Draper, and the next day being March 3d wee got safe home to Boston, where I found my aged and tender mother and my Dear and only Child[1] in good health with open arms redy to receive me, and my Kind relations and friends flocking in to welcome mee and hear the

[1] Elizabeth, Madam Knight's only child, then about seventeen, has already been mentioned in the preface and in a note. In the inventory of her effects, taken after her death, appear the items ;

story of my transactions and travails I having this day bin five months from home and now I cannot fully express my Joy and Satisfaction. But desire sincearly to adore my Great Benefactor for thus graciously carying forth and returning in safety his unworthy handmaid.

a negro man and woman; an Indian man; silver plate £234, 13s; several rings and other jewelry. Acquittances given to the administratrix of her estate are signed by the following persons: Sarah Bass of Boston, widow Mary Bassett of Boston, William Wyer and Elinor, his wife of Charlestown, Robert Luist, shopkeeper, of Charlestown, James Fluker and his wife Elizabeth of Charlestown, Thomas Cheever and his wife Abigail of Chelsea. Miss Caulkins' *History of New London*, 365, and her letter to W. R. D.

Note to Providence ferry, page 26.

Judge Staples, author of the *Annals of Providence*, is of opinion that the oldest ferry over the Seekonk river was at Narrow Passage, so called, near where the bridge now is. The riding-over place across Moshassack river was at the foot of Steeple Street. See further, *Annals of Providence*, 196, 611. A glance at the map shows us that Madam Knight does not mention all the rivers or streams she must have passed through. E. R. P.

Sarah Knight

INDEX.

Adams, Eliphalet, his funeral discourse on Rev. Gurdon Saltonstall, 45.
Alfogeos, 57.
Antiquarian subjects unfashionable, 16.
Apponarg, 26.
Ayrault, a French Huguenot physician, 36.
Baptist church in New York, 69.
Bass, Sarah, 85.
Bassett, Mary, 85.
Belcher, Rev. Joseph, graduated and ordained, 20.
Billings' tavern, where, 20, 22.
Bowery the, 70.
Bradford, Joseph, joint purchaser of land with Madam Knight, viii.
Building, style of, in New York, 67.
Bull's garrison house, 36.
Burroughs, Thomas, a merchant of New York, 63, 70.
Caulkins, Miss Frances R., her History of N. L., vii; letter, 42,
Champlin's tavern, 38.
Changes since 1704, 17.
Charlestown, 26, 36.
Cheever, Thomas, 85.
Christophers, Sarah, ix; Mary, 81.
Clark, Ann, Madam Knight's maid, vii.
Coeymans house mentioned, 67.
Connecticut, boundaries and description of, 79.
Cornbury, Lord, 60, 68,
Crocker, Mrs Hannah Mather, x.
Cross' mills, formerly Davell's, 36.
Darcy, Lord, story, of, 64.

INDEX.

Davell spelled Devil, 37.
Davell's mills, now Cross' mills, 36, 38.
Deadman's spring, 36.
Deane, William R., his article on Madam Knight, iv.
Dedham, 19; causeway at, 84.
Devil's Foot rock, celebrated among the Indians, 33.
Divorce, freedom of in Connecticut among whites and Indians, 55.
Douglas road near New London, 47.
Draper, ———, 184.
East Greenwich, 26.
Election day, 59.
Exeter, 35.
Fairfield, 61.
Fare at inns, 25, 39, 42, 45, 48, 61, 62, 73, 75, 82.
Fluker, James, 85.
Flyboat, 66.
Fort neck and Indian fort at that place, 37.
Franklin, Dr., said to have been a scholar of Madam Knight, vi.
French physician, 35.
Grafton, Remember, former wife of Richard Knight, v.
Guilford, 49.
Haven's tavern, where situated, 33.
Heathcote, Col. Caleb, 74.
Hunt's river, 29.
Huguenots, settlement, 35.
Immersion alluded to, 28.
Indians near New Haven, condition and customs of, 54; crimes how punished, 55; mourning of, 56; eagerness for rum, *ib.*; which the merchants water for them, *ib.*
Introduction to first edition, 15.
Kemble, John, his will, iv.
Journal, when printed, iii; how preserved, ix; destroyed, x.
Kemble, Thomas, father of Madam Knight, his residence and business, iv; house in Boston demolished, site how occupied, *ib.*; his death and gravestone, v; house sold, vi.
Killingsworth, 48.
Kingston, new road through, 26, 35.

INDEX.

Knight, Elizabeth, only child of Madam Knight, her birth, marriage, death and gravestone, vii; presents her mother's inventory, x; inventory of her effects, 85.

Knight, Madam, her birth, iii; parents, iv; marriage, v; school, vi; sold her house, inscription on a pane of glass, *ib.*; her title how acquired, *ib.* and 15; removal to Norwich and New London, vii; presents a cup to the church and pew voted to her, viii; presented for selling strong drink, *ib.*; purchaser of land, *ib.*; pewholder in New London, ix; kept an inn on the Norwich road, *ib.*; her death, and the inventory of her estate, *ib.*; a witness to papers, x ; her character and accuracy, xi; her gravestone, xii; why called Madam Knight, 15; sets out from Boston, 19; arrives at Dedham, *ib.*; visits Mr. Belcher, 20; reaches Billings', 22; goes on to the post's second stage, 25; proceeds with her third guide, crosses Providence ferry and comes to a river at Pawtuxet, 26; fords Mascachuge river, 29; arrives at Haven's tavern, 33; sets out for Kingston, 35; reaches Devill's, 37; Champlin's, 38; and Pawcatuc river, 39; stays at Saxton's, in Stonington, 42; arrives at New London, 44; at Mrs. Prentis' and at Rev. Gurdon Saltonstall's, 45; arrives at Saybrook ferry, 47; Killingsworth, 48; Guilford, and New Haven, 49; observation upon New Haven, 49 to 59; sets out for New York, 61; arrives at Stratford ferry, Fairfield and Norwalk, 61; Rye, 62; New Rochelle and New York, 63; description of New York, 66 to 70; goes from New York, 71; reaches Eastchester, 72; New Rochelle, 73; Mamaroneck, *ib.*; Horseneck, 74; Norwalk and Fairfield, 75; mode of paying parson's salary, 76; passes through Stratford and stays at Milford, 77; and arrives at New Haven, 79; goes from New Haven to New London, 81; crosses to Groton, 82; and goes to Stonington and to Havens', *ib.*; arrives at Dedham and at Boston, 84.

Knight, Richard, husband of Madam Knight, his business, his former marriage, his death abroad, v.

Knight of the Oracle, 22.

Latimer's, Miss, road leading by, 47.

Lean to, 24.

Lecture days, 52.

Liveen will, the, 60.
Livingston, Col. John, married to Elizabeth Knight, vii; purchaser of land, viii; his farm, ix; his former wife, 81; his residence and death, *ib*.
Luist, Capt. Robert, accompanies Madam Knight to Dedham, 19, 85.
McCoon's mills, 26.
Marriages at an early age, 53; singular custom at, *ib*.
Mascachuge river, hazardous crossing of, 29.
Mather, Hannah, became the owner of Madam Knight's house, vi.
Mather, Increase, vii.
Mather, Samuel, scholar of Madam Knight, vi.
Maxon, Jesse, town clerk of Westerly, 39.
Maxwell, William P., his house, 33.
Milford, 77.
Mosaic law the rule for courts, 51.
Muscheetoes, 41.
Narragansett country, 29: controversy as to the meaning of, 34.
Neale, Thomas, received letters patent for establishing a post office, 19.
New Haven, 49; laws and church government of, 49; character of the people, *ib.*; the strictness of the laws, 50; amusements, 52; marriages, 53; oysters, *ib.*; indulgence to slaves, 54; Indian customs, 55; mode of traffic, 56.
New London ferry, arrival at, account of, 43.
New York, description of, 66; style of building, 67; fort, 68; arrival of Lord Cornbury, 68; Churches in, *ib.*; character and dress of the people, 69; diversions, 70.
Niantic river, crossing at, 46.
Norwalk, the derivation of the name, 61; bridge at, 75.
Oysters, abundance of, 53.
Papillion, Peter, purchaser of Madam Knight's house, vi.
Paper, price of, 66.
Parade at New London, 44.
Parismus, by Edward Forde, 22.
Pawcatuc bridge, 26; river, riding-over place at, 39.
Pawtuxet, river at, 26.
Pequot road, 26.
Pieces of eight, 20, 21, 56.

INDEX.

Pierpont, Rev. James, 80.
Point Judith salt ponds, 36.
Polly, ——, and his daughter, 43.
Post, the western, its route, 19; where met, 25.
Post office established, 19; chief in Connecticut, 25.
Potter, E. R., 26.
Poverty of a family, 40.
Prentis, Mrs. John, her tavern, 45.
Prout, Capt. John, 63; his marriage, 81.
Providence ferry, 26, 85.
Punctuation of the journal, 17.
Quakers, 21; meeting house in New York, 69; singing, 77.
Reding, showing the way to, 24.
Richards, Capt. John, 83.
Riverhead of the Niantic, 47.
Rogers, Samuel, 81.
Rogerenes, the, 81.
Rope ferry over Niantic, 46.
Route through Rhode Island, 26; through Stonington, 42; to Saybrook, 47.
Sad-colored, meaning of, 24.
Saltonstall, Rev. Gurdon, when born, ordained and chosen governor, 45; his death and character, ib.; his house, ib., 81.
Saugatuck river, 75.
Saxton, Capt. Joseph, formerly of Boston, his house, 42.
Saybrook ferry, 47.
Seats in the "meeting-house" how assigned, viii.
Shaw's riding-over place, 39.
Shooting at the target, 52.
Slaves, anecdote about, 51; indulgence towards, 53; arbitration with, 54.
Spelling, the original preserved, 17.
Stonington, the route through, 42.
Stratford ferry, 61, 77.
Sugar loaf hill, 36.
Taxes, paid in wheat, 56.
Tiles, use of, in houses, 67.
Trade, how carried on, 56.

Training days, 52.
Trarice, Elizabeth, mother of Madam Knight, iv ; her death and gravestone, v.
Travel, increased speed of, xii.
Trowbridge, Caleb, Madam Knight a witness to papers on the settlement of his estate, x.
Trowbridge, Thomas, his birth, 61 ; his parents, 81.
Tower hill, 26, 35, 36.
Updike, Lodowick, his house where situated, 38 ; Madam Knight passes near it, 39.
Vendue in New York, 66, 69.
Vesey, William, clergyman in New York, 68.
Wakefield, 26, 36.
Wampom used for change, 56.
Webb, Joseph, clergyman at Fairfield, 76.
Wedding Place, the, 70.
Wetmore, Mrs. Ichabod, x.
Wheeler house in New London, 46.
Wheeler, Joshua, Madam Knight's guide to New Haven, 46, 49.
Wickford, 26.
Winthrop, Fitz-John, Governor of Connecticut, his popularity and character, 80.
Winthrop, Mary, wife of Col. Livingston, her death and burial, 82.
Wyer, William, 85.

CPSIA information can be obtained
at www.ICGtesting.com
Printed in the USA
BVHW041803120719
553314BV00015B/225/P